Playground
SCIENCE

By Elizabeth Paren

CELEBRATION PRESS
Pearson Learning Group

Contents

Science in Action

A playground is a great place to see science in action. It's full of movement. People run, slide, play with balls, and fly kites. Seesaws go up and down, bicycles race by, and swings swing. What makes these things move the way they do?

Things move when they are pushed or pulled. These pushes and pulls are called **forces**. Forces can make objects move or stop. If we kick a ball with a light tap, it rolls slowly. If we kick it harder, the force of the kick makes the ball go farther and faster.

We cannot always see forces. However, we can see the movements they cause. Learning about forces helps us understand why things move the way they do.

Why Does a Ball Drop?

When you toss a ball, the ball is pushed into the air. The push is the force that starts the ball moving. The harder it is pushed, the farther it will go.

The ball won't go through the air forever, though. It will drop back to the ground because of the pull of **gravity**. Gravity is the force that pulls things back to Earth. Without gravity, the ball would fly away into space.

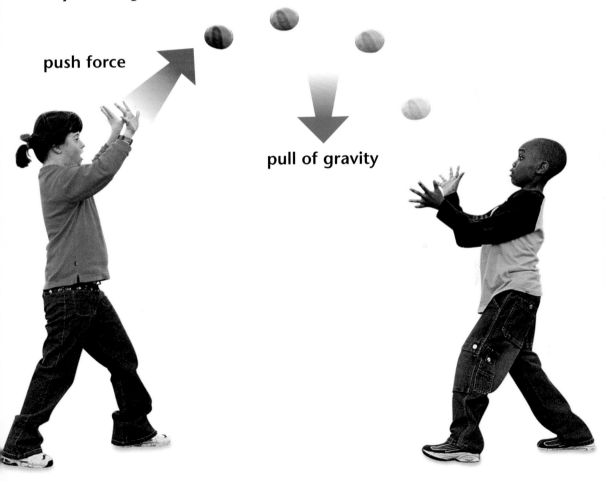

push force

pull of gravity

How Does a Kite Fly?

If gravity pulls everything toward the Earth, how does a kite stay up in the air? There is a force that works against gravity to make the kite fly. Wind provides that force.

Wind pushes against the kite, creating **pressure**. There is less pressure above the kite than below it. The difference in pressure is called **lift**. Lift makes the kite rise.

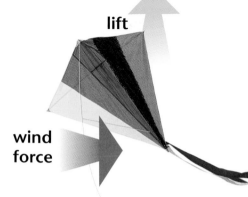

lift

wind force

Why Does a Seesaw Go Up and Down?

When two children sit on a seesaw, they try to **balance** each other. When one child pushes away from the ground and against gravity, that end of the seesaw goes up. The other end of the seesaw is pushed down, helped by gravity.

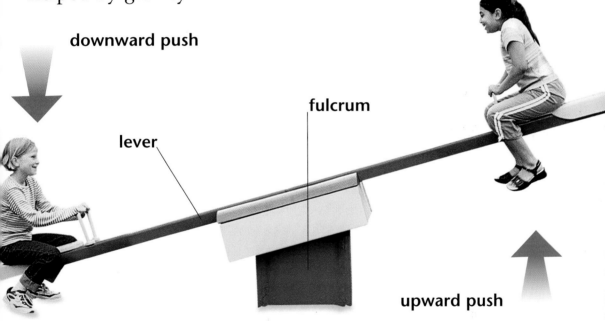

downward push

fulcrum

lever

upward push

Seesaws are **simple machines** that change the direction of a force. In the picture above, the seesaw changes the upward push on the right into a downward push on the left. When the child on the left pushes, this becomes reversed. Simple machines that move this way are called **levers**. A lever turns about a point called a **fulcrum**.

How Does a Slide Work?

Gravity pulls a person down a slide. The steeper a slide is, the faster the person will go. At the end, the slide levels off. **Friction** slows a person down so he or she can travel down the slide safely.

A slide is an example of a simple machine called an **inclined plane**. An inclined plane has a flat, slanted surface.

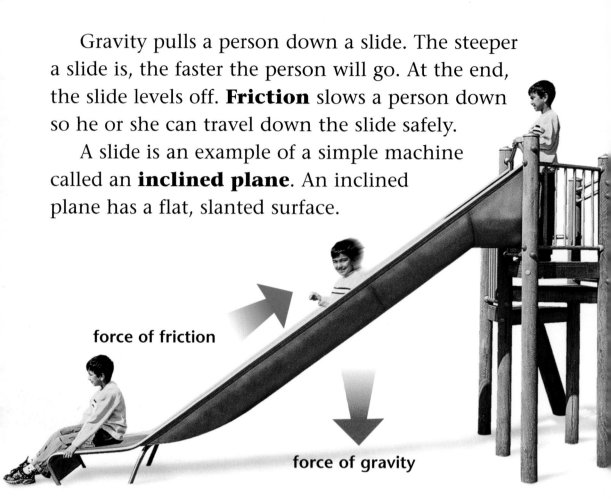

force of friction

force of gravity

Ramps to the Rescue
A **ramp** is also an inclined plane. Pushing an object up a ramp is easier than lifting the object straight up. When you use a ramp, you lift the object a little at a time. You don't have to push or pull your hardest all at once.

Friction keeps a person from moving too fast down a slide.

Making a slide's surface smooth helps to reduce the amount of friction on the slide. Friction happens because all surfaces have bumps and pits on them. When two surfaces come together, these bumps and pits rub against each other. On a slide, the slide's surface and a person's clothing rub together. This creates friction, which slows the person down. The force of friction is weak because the slide is smooth.

Why Do Swings Swing?

Most movements are caused by a combination of forces. Swinging is one example. When a person swings, there are many forces at work. The first force is a push that makes the swing begin to move forward. The harder the push, the higher the swing goes.

The chains or ropes on the swing provide a second force. This force changes the direction of the swing. It makes the swing arc up.

forward force

1. Pushing the swing makes it move forward.

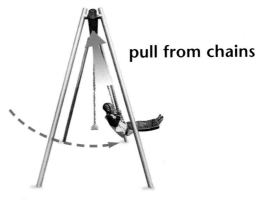

pull from chains

2. The chains pull up, moving the swing in an arc.

gravity

3. Gravity pulls the swing down.

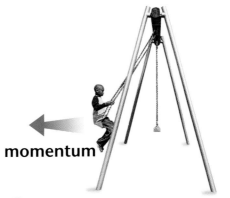

momentum

4. Momentum makes the swing continue moving backward.

Gravity slows the swing, stops it, and pulls it back down. The swing gains speed. It goes past the starting point because of its **momentum**. Momentum is the amount of motion that an object has. It takes force to change an object's momentum.

Force is needed to keep the swing moving. Without it, friction will slow the swing and make it stop. The force to keep a swing moving can come from someone pushing the swing or from the rider swinging his or her legs.

What Makes a Bicycle Go?

A bicycle moves by many forces working together. Pushing on the pedals turns a **gear**. A gear is a wheel that has teeth around the edges. A chain around the gear moves when the gear moves.

The chain also fits around a gear on the back wheel. A push on the pedals makes both gears turn. When the back gear turns, so does the back wheel. Friction between the back tire and the road moves the bicycle forward.

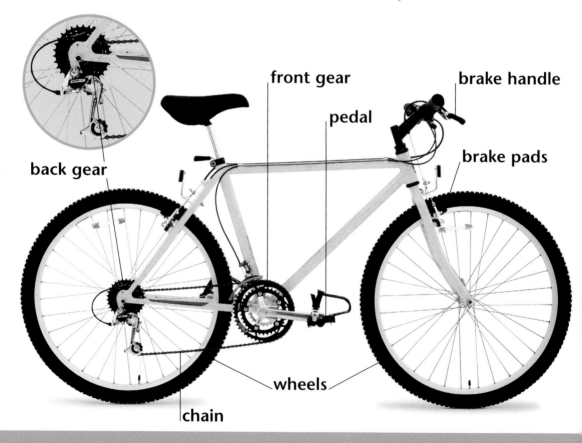

back gear

front gear

pedal

brake handle

brake pads

wheels

chain

The turning wheels and friction make the bicycle roll instead of slide. The rough tread of the tires increases friction, which helps the tires grip the road.

The rider pulls the brake levers to stop the bicycle. The levers make the brake blocks rub against the rims of the wheels. This produces friction on the wheels and stops the bike.

More Wheels on the Go
Riders of skateboards and skates need to push against the ground with their feet to make the wheels turn.

Playground Science

A playground is the perfect place to watch things move and to begin to understand forces. You have read how gravity and other forces help you slide, swing, bounce balls, and fly kites. You've discovered that some of the things you play on are simple machines that use and change the forces around you. What other activities do you see at playgrounds? Have some fun and explore the forces behind them!

Glossary

balance   to keep steady and even

forces   pushes and pulls that make things move, change speed, and change direction

friction   what happens when two surfaces rub together; it slows down movement

fulcrum   the point around which a lever turns

gear   a wheel with teeth evenly spaced along its edge

gravity   the force that pulls all objects toward each other; Earth's gravity pulls things down toward its center

inclined plane   a simple machine with a slanted, flat surface

lever   a simple machine; pushing down on one end makes the other end go up

lift   a force that makes an object rise in the air

momentum   the amount of motion that an object has

pressure   a force pushing against a surface

ramp   a road, walkway, or other surface in the form of an inclined plane

simple machine   a tool that changes the direction or the strength of a force

Index